THE DESIGN, CONSTRUCTION, AND OPERATION OF A MOTOR POWER

CA RE.R . .L DY.. .C.. .R

.L..

P.. .. .

. .I .III .

G .. G. . .. .I.

.. .

.. ..

. .. .UR I . .. . T . ..

.or t. . .. .. .

. . . . . .

.. . .

L. . . L E. G .

.. 25, 1918.

TABLE OF CONTENTS.

1.

*   OBJECT   *

The object of this thesis is the construction
of a horse power meter to be used in connection
with a rear wheel absorption dynamometer, for the
measurement of the horse power delivered at the
rear wheel of an automobile.

*   DEFINITION   *

A horse-power meter is a mechanism, having:-
speed registering capabilities, which ... ve s i-
dicator across a ...; a i ter ... distributing s-
illiaries ... ...
r tot... ... ...
ments of ... ...
to the ... ...
r ..l .

3.

*   . . . . . .   *

This thesis is   third one to be pre-
serted o. the s..est .. . . . . o...r .. .r,
which is to be .sed for . .s .ri. t. .. . .r
delivered at 1 o .ear . . . . . . .o . .io.

. .. or. .. / . . . .
a h.rse .o e. .ter . . . . io. . . . .
c. t . . . .
of 1. .. . .
t. .1 .. . .
t.ere. . . . .
t.. . . . .

. . . .

. . . .

. . . . e . .

. . . .

. . . .

. . . .

t.. . . . .

r..er . . . .

t.. . . . .

. . . . .

The remainder of the time at their [illegible]
spent [illegible]
[illegible]
[illegible]
[illegible]
[illegible]
[illegible]
[illegible]
[illegible]
After [illegible]
[illegible]
[illegible]

DESCRIPTION OF VEHICLE.

THE AUTOMOBILE. The automobile chassis
which will be used in this work is a ....
1911 model. The engine is a four cylinder,
four cycle, 4-1/2" bore, 5 1/2" t.....
model ...-A, and is rated at ....
The cylinders are cast singly, and are b.....
to the crank case. The ..di. ....
ciated by a brake test, ...
fo et ..... is ...li.......................
o braking ....
s .... is ....
sir .... The .... is ....
t e ....:-

        1. First   11.75   to 1
        2. Second   ....   to 1
        3. Third   ....   to 1   (direct)
        4. Reverse   1.23   to 1

The propelle. . . . is ....a t .. ar
torque case, ...versal joint. ... e
rear axel is on the full-floting t ..e. The
wheels are ade to carr. 5-1/2" x 36" tires.

THE DYNAMOMETER. The dynamometer to be used
in this test is an ALDEN water dynamometer. The
dynamometer proper comprises; a cast iron disk
firmly keyed to a 2" chrome nickle steel shaft;
a copper friction disk placed on each side of
the cast iron disk; and a cast iron casing, with
stiffeners (ribs), on the outside, which casing
encloses the two sets of disks, and holds the
water which produces the pressure on the friction
disks. A brake is adjusted to the casing so
the torque developed in the dynamometer to the
diaphram of an oil reservoir. The water enters
and leaves the casing thru 1/." pipes, and serv
the double purpose, of producing pressure on the
friction disks, and carrying away the heat
developed by the absorbtion of the power.

The shaft carrying the dynamometer is
in four large bearings, and on the shaft between
each pair of bearings is bolted split pulley
wheels 8' - 10" in diameter, and 3-1'2" across
the face. The rear wheels of the automobile will
be backed onto the pulleys for the test. The

general layout of the apparatus is shown in fig. 1.

THE OIL RESERVOIR. The oil reservoir, to which the torque developed in the dynamometer will be transmitted, consists of a flanged cast iron bowl 2-3/8" deep, 12" internal diameter, and 16" across the face of the flange. A corrugated copper disk is fastened down on the top of the bowl by means of a cast iron ring fitted with 12 5/8" bolts. Within the center of the bowl, there is a small pedestal for preventing the diaphragm from being subjected to too great a depression. A cast iron disk, having a spherical bottom, rests on the diaphragm and serves to distribute the pressure produced by the torque arm.

The dynamometer and oil pressure reservoir are mounted on a test rack placed in a pit which is just deep enough to permit the rim of the large pulley wheels to project about an inch above the floor line. This arrangement facilitates the handling of any car which is to be tested.

THE HORSE-POWER METER. The horse-power

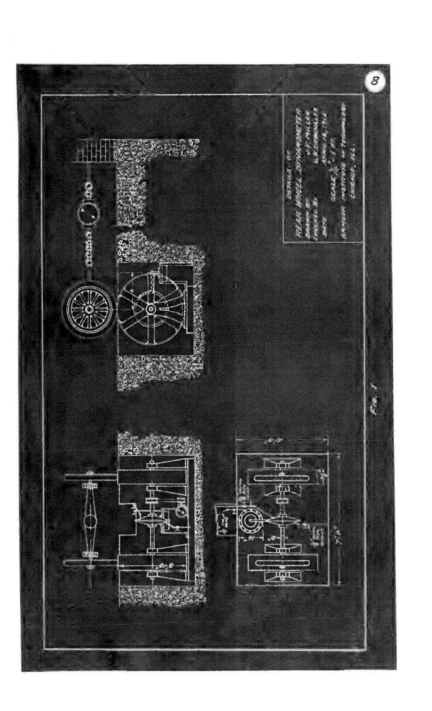

meter mechanisms are contained within an alumi-
num casing. The tachometer mechanism, see
fig. 2), as three sets of gears; 1, 2 and 3,
and 4, which give the following gear ratios:-

    1. Ratio of 1 to 2 & 3 is 2 to 1

    2. Ratio of 2 3 to 4 is 2 to 1.

Each set of gears is mounted on a shaft which
projects beyond the case, and which passes through
a sleeve on the outside of the casing. The
sleeve is turned and the rotation of the
flexible shaft so that each may be securely
fastened to the sleeve of this gears. In this
way, each gear can be connected, and that
speed of rotation to the various shaft, of
gears to be which cause to turn either the indicator needle, or a mirror reel on the rim,
or otherwise be shafted.

    The thread, which carries the indicating
needle, connects to the circumference of a reel
and passes over two small pulley wheels, mounted
at each end of the upper frame or a shaft on

paper chart travels.

The upper drum is turned by a small puller wheel fastened to one end of the drum shaft. The pulley is rotated by a wisted string which is attached to a brass float resting on the surface of a mercury manometer. The mercury level rises and falls as the pressure in the oil reservoir increases or decreases. The pressure in the oil reservoir is transmitted to the mercury in the horse-power meter thru an eighth inch pipe. This is filled with oil, and connects the reservoir with the manometer.

FIG. 2.

CALIBRATION OF TORQUE, AND SPEED REGISTING APP'

OIL P. ESSU... ...GE VAL.. he oil reservoir
diaphragm which is to e used i e torque
recording mechanism was calibrated in the .o.lo i
manner:-

the load was pla ed on the spherical
plate, o. t e coi. th dia. ragm, hich
su ported a .is. el er, .. hi e
plazed cast i.. oints, hi i ... ..
4. to .. pounds e.. . he .tl .
tie .. .., .. ins.ct.. a .at ..o.
plate .or .l. hin the h. &. .. il
reservoir .. .ou. .t. . 1'-" power
nipl.. to .. ... h .re. .. . ..
A .li .o.. .l. , as. i.. ..
Co.. ...... .o. h.., .t . .. ..e
of tuese ... .i. . .. . . .
were take. as t.e .ne caliorati. vata.
Aft r the calivri i. a. ide, .
wei. ts .hich hec .. ... h.h. . b .e.
were eigo c.a .. .. . plate. scale.

The results of this calibration are given on the next page.

Note: Before calibrating the copper diaphragm, all the air was expelled by running oil thru the reservoir, and piping.

DATA FOR OIL RESERVOIR CALIBRATION CURVE.

Load applied on diaphragm in pounds:-	Difference in consecutive readings:- (In. Hg.)	Summation of consecutive readings:- (In. Hg.)
0	0.00	0.00
26	1.85	1.85
86	4.85	6.70
135	3.91	10.61
187	3.11	13.72
237	2.94	16.66
287	2.78	19.44
342	3.03	22.47
392	2.65	25.12
441	2.41	27.53
492	2.47	30.00
542	2.31	32.31
592	2.24	34.55
642	1.98	36.53
693	1.77	38.30
748	1.52	39.82
798	1.59	41.41

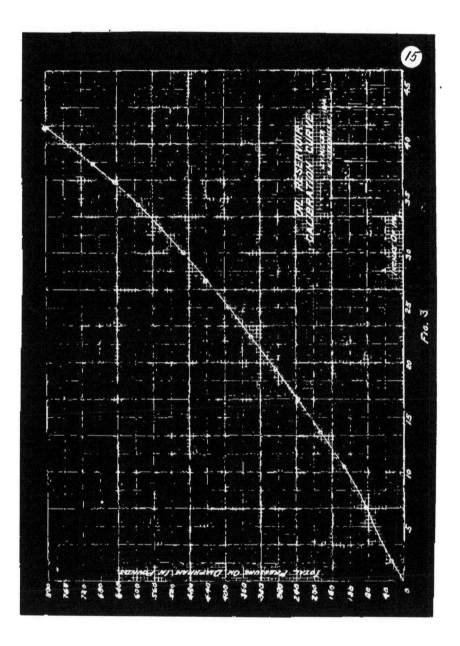

OIL RESERVOIR
CALIBRATION CURVE

FIG. 3

HORSE-POWER METER TACHOMETER. The tachometer
for the horse-power meter was calibrated in the
machine shop in the following manner:-

The thick bottom of the rear housing A,
(see fig. 2), was clamped in a vise, just
firmly enough to prevent vibration; then,
one end of a length of flexible shafting
was coupled to the shaft supporting rear A,
and the other end was fastened in the jaws
of a universal chuck, fastened to the spindle of a high speed lathe. It read, neatly
wound on drum J, had a center supported at its
free end and was placed along the spindle in
a steel angle plate and in a vertical position.
As the speed of rotation increases, the plate
of the governor weight tends to assume a position normal to the axis of the shaft.
At any constant speed, the position of the
governor weight makes an angle so that it
angle it remains, because the force of
the centrifugal motion is balanced by
the tension in the governor spring. The
motion of the governor weight is transmitted

to the wheel to which the weighted three
is attached, and this causes the same to
rise along the scale.

DATA FOR TACHOMETER CALIBRATION CURVE.

The travel of the key along the scale, at various speeds was as follows:-

Revolutions Per Minute. (For gear 2 & 3)	Lift of Three (In inches
550	1.24
800	3.81
1100	6.21
1175	6.84
1500	9.79
2100	14.27
2200	17.22

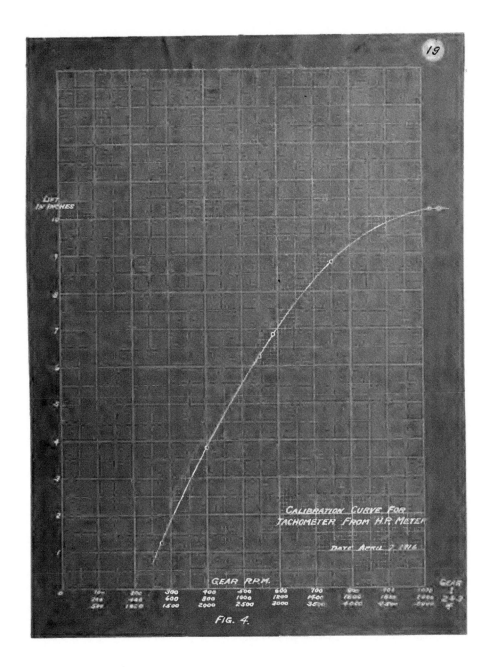

FIG. 4.

CONSTRUCTION OF TRANSMISSION GEARS.

The proper number of teeth for the gear
which was to mesh with the split gear on the dynamometer shaft, and give the right amount of travel
of the indicating pointer, was determined as
follows:-

The maximum movement of the circumference of the tachometer wheel C, (See
Fig. 2), as determined in the calibration
test, was 14.88 inches, at a speed of
r.p.m. of the governor shaft L. The most
regular position of the curve lies between one or indications of pointing C and
C inches of lift. This would represent
a travel of eight inches corresponds to a unit.
The speed of rotation of shaft L, 3 as
shown on the chart, corresponds to a
lift of inches, so that ....

The .... rate of rotation of the
engine of the .... LM gear shaft L
.... direct drive .... the ....
would be a little rate of 1 ....

or 514.2? ......

The speed of the pulley wheels on
the generator shaft is .... tional to
the product of the speed ... the .... wheels
and the inverse ratio of t ... per...
diameters; .... is t.e s... ....
of ... ...

(D_r^2 ÷ D_) × 214.2. or ...

... 1lt ...
shaft is ... teeth, 15 dia..t... ....
and the ... which will ... the ... ft
...yi... ...rs 2 ... r..t... ...
when th. ... l't ... ...es "1. ill
have (32. ÷ 135.. × 62 = 1..7 or 1£ teeth.

22.

FIG. 5.

FIG. 6.

24.

FIG. 7.

25

PRELIMINARY RUN.

After we had bolted the H. P. meter to the top of table 2, (see fig. 8), and coupled, to sleeve S, the flexible shaft leading from the pinion gear operated by the dynamometer shaft, we backed the car on to the pulley wheels .. Two pieces of cable attached to a spring scale, having a capacity of 1000 pounds, prevented the car from run in off the pulley wheels, when the gears were put in mesh. A scale was put in to check the monometer mechanism of the H.I. meter while it is being calibrated.

As soon as everything had been connected up, we started the engine, and put the car on first gear, allowing it to idle slowly, so as to permit a careful watch to be kept on all parts of the apparatus. Everything appeared to be working as it should, and we then stopped the engine so as to enable a careful inspection to be made of all moving parts. No faults were found during the inspection, so we started

the engine again. The engine started with a
jerk, then almost stopped, and then ran with
a jerky motion. We shut the engine down and
made a very thorough search to ... out ...
... we found that practically all the
gear teeth of the idler gear, which ...
between the split gear and the pinion, had ...
stri ... while ra ... ... to t
water ... n c ... ridti ... ...
d ... ... or pressure prevented
the en ... from starting smoothly, and the
... i ... t trl ... l a ... t ire ... ... t
rear. ... ...
i ... g ... l t ... ... re ... ...
... ... , s ... t ...
... ... t ... ... w ... ... y. ... ...
e ... ... wheels. the ... te
pres ... ... th ... d ... at r,
without ... ... l ... g ... th ... ... sugges-
tion ... ... rt .

automobile for more than a half hour of con-
ti... r...t r, ...ting
un... ... ... st t... ... ...
he...i ... ... li...e ... ... s ... .
finall; ... ...el t is ... ... ck ... ...
a 1'" cor...r tr...e fro t...e ...o ...te. ...
line to t...e re...ntor, a d corre...ting t...e ...t-
l...t ... ...e overflo... ...i... a pine le...i... t... ...
g...er. ... t...is ...e, t...e r...di... ...t...as a... ... t
...l... of ... t...ter, ...ver so ...t es t... st ...,
... t...e ...i...oul... l...e ...rated contin... ...l;
...i...t ...v...r tir...

FIG. 8.

CALIBRATION OF FORCE-INDICATOR.

The tachometer, and manometer mechanisms, although once calibrated while separated from the case, gave data for determining, approximately the proper length of mercury manometer for th . . . meter, and the correct ratio of gear teeth for the pinion driving the flexible shaft. After the two mechanisms had been brought together, and properly connected to the remaining test apparatus, it was necessary to calibrate the two mechanisms, again, in order that a chart might be drawn for the meter.

MANOMETER CALIBRATION. The flexible shafting was disengaged from the driving pinion, and the engine put on direct drive. Water pressure in the manometer was regulated by means of the inlet valve, and a series of points read, true . . . the shaft . . . the correction in . . . los . . , as obtained from the sliding scale, recorded. The total . . , inches, corresponding to the recorded pressure, were summed up in table 1, and curve A, (see fig. . was plotted with this data.

30.

TACHOMETER CALIBRATION. The flexible shafting
was again connected with the driving engine, and
the inlet, and outlet valves .... of,
and 1/2 turn .... of the ....
o air at .... ive. .... of .... t,
(see fig. 2) ....
r. to .... ree
... of .... ist ....
t...l.... .... of th...... ....
of ft. ....t.
.... in ....

......le , ... i ....
.... , ...
on a dis ...., ...
cl s.....d. hi .... t. .l. ... .
fig. 1..

la ....
in fig. ...... fi. . l.; t.e l.l... in lo. on the
copper .... f.... l., . t.
inches o .....l... ....
on t e ...., ... t......... ...

... . , ...r ...
meter ....plott. .... in
t.....

TABLE I.

Vertical travel of paper over drum in inches.	Brake load in pounds.
0.0	0.0
1.7	38.0
3.5	65.0
5.13	111.0
5.77	126.5
6.64	160.0
7.05	180.0
7.50	188.0
8.23	229.0
9.22	278.0

TABLE 2.

Horizontal travel of indicating pointing in inches	Governor shaft (D) R.P.M.	Rear wheel R.P.M.
2.02	620	96
3.16	730	117
3.92	798	122
5.03	898	141
6.53	1112	176
7.51	1260	198
8.51	1460	230
9.64	2035	285

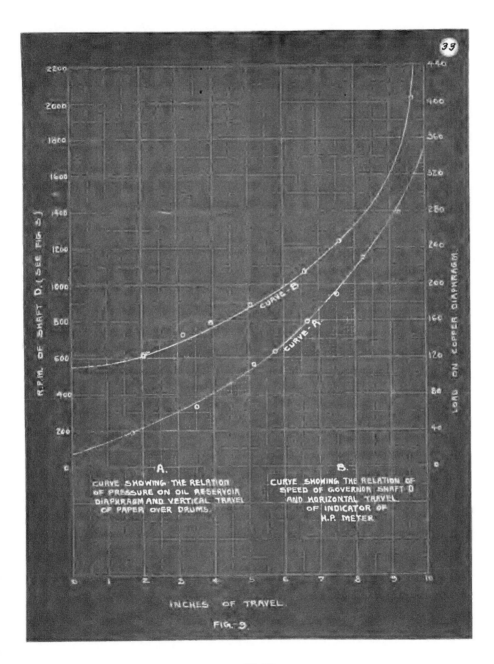

33

A.
CURVE SHOWING THE RELATION
OF PRESSURE ON OIL RESERVOIR
DIAPHRAGM AND VERTICAL TRAVEL
OF PAPER OVER DRUMS.

B.
CURVE SHOWING THE RELATION OF
SPEED OF GOVERNOR SHAFT D
AND HORIZONTAL TRAVEL
OF INDICATOR OF
H.P. METER

CURVE-B

CURVE-A

R.P.M. OF SHAFT D.(SEE FIG. 2.)

LOAD ON COPPER DIAPHRAGM.

INCHES OF TRAVEL.

FIG.-9.

TABLE 3.

Length of brake arm equals radius of pulley wheel = 23"

$$D.H.P. = \frac{2 \quad L \cdot N}{33000} = \frac{2 \times 23 \quad W \cdot N}{33000 \times 12} = 0.000365 \cdot W \cdot N$$

R. P. M. of dynamometer wheels = N = 28 x 15 x R.P.M. of

(D)   N = 0.121 x R.P.M. of (D)

R.P.M. (D)	Load on copper diaphragm in pounds.					
	40	80	120	160	200	240
	H.P. developed at rear wheels.					
200	0.354	0.707	1.06	1.414	1.767	2.12
400	0.707	1.414	2.12	2.828	3.534	4.24
600	1.062	2.121	3.18	4.242	5.301	6.36
800	1.414	2.828	4.24	5.656	7.068	8.48
1000	1.767	3.535	5.30	7.07	8.835	10.60
1200	2.12	4.242	6.36	8.484	10.602	12.72
1400	2.478	4.949	7.42	9.898	12.369	14.84
1600	2.832	5.656	8.48	11.312	14.136	16.96
1800	3.186	6.363	9.54	12.726	15.903	19.08
2000	3.54	7.07	10.60	14.14	17.67	21.20

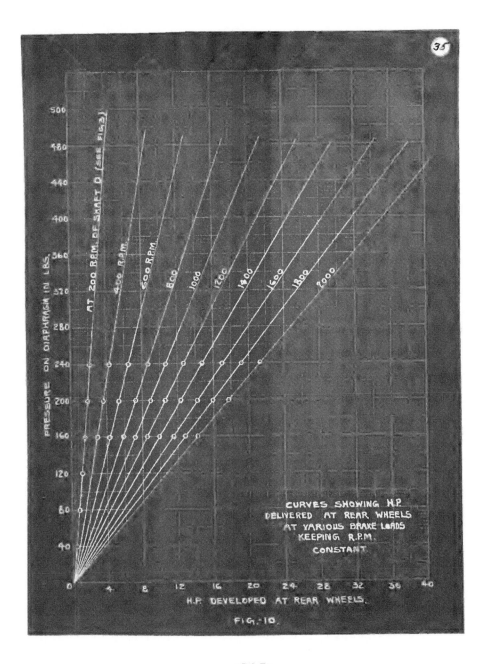

CURVES SHOWING H.P.
DELIVERED AT REAR WHEELS
AT VARIOUS BRAKE LOADS
KEEPING R.P.M.
CONSTANT.

FIG. 10.

I.M.P.	200		400		600		800		1000	
	Brake load	Vertical travel in inches	Brake load	Vertical travel in inches	Brake load	Vertical travel in inches	Brake load	Vertical travel in inches	Brake load	Vertical travel in inches
1.0	116	5.1	5.	2.4	36	1.65	28	1.25	22	0.9
2.0			114	5.0	7?		6.		4.	2.15
3.0	50	10.05	174	6.9	116	5.05	66	3.90	70	
5.0			90	3.8	192	7.55	142		116	
6.0			45?					6.06	182	7.1
8.0					770	9.92				9.96
10.0							545			
14.0										
20.0										
25.0										
30.0										
35.0										

37

R.P.M. of (L)

R.P.M.	1200 Brake load	1200 Vertical travel in inches	1400 Brake load	1400 Vertical travel in inches	1600 Brake load	1600 Vertical travel in inches	1800 Brake load	1800 Vertical travel in inches	200 Brake load
1.0	18	0.70	33	1.5	30	1.35	26	1.10	22
2.0	38	1.75	50	2.3	44	2.05	38	1.75	35
3.0	59	2.75	84	3.8	72	3.3	65	3.0	63
5.0	98	4.40	130	3.8	113	4.98	101	4.5	90
8.0	152	6.26	130	5.6	113	4.98	101	4.5	90
8.0	152	6.26	130	5.6	113	4.98	101	4.5	90
10.0	194	7.4	163	6.6	140	5.9	126	5.45	114
14.0	286	9.25	246	8.5	213	7.95	190	7.34	171
20.0	380		327	9.8	262	9.20	252	8.65	227
25.0			408		352	10.00	316	9.43	284
30.0					425		378		339
35.0									396

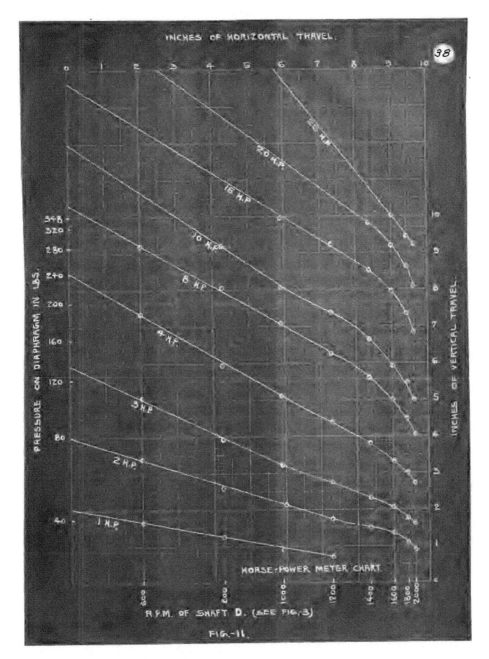

INCHES OF HORIZONTAL TRAVEL.

PRESSURE ON DIAPHRAGM IN LBS.

INCHES OF VERTICAL TRAVEL.

HORSE-POWER METER CHART.

R.P.M. OF SHAFT D. (SEE FIG. 3)

FIG.-11.

CONCLUSION.

The results which we have obtained with the
H.P. meter have been very encouraging, and indicate
the H. P. meter can be used reliably in a commercial
machine.

We would recommend that a more suitable telescopic joint, with level springs, on the slide shaft, and a more adequate friction driving connection ... [illegible] ... reduce ... faults, ... will ... in ... high speed, ... that something might be done in ... to the ... friction ... as it ... on a universal joint ...

... should be ... a drum ... [illegible] ... diameters ... s ... of friction ... the ... This friction, although very small, did the tendency for the chart to slip on the drums.

Finally, we wish to state, that if a small jet of light machine oil be squirted into the H.P. meter tube, and that the level of the oil is at the

t a half inch below the top of the float, the float

l rise, a... ....

ing a t...e...t -words at...

e are greatly i   to essers nesoh

erd urtley for the east   e

lave   t

c hi

1